WORDS TO INSPIRE YOU TO DREAM

Copyright © 2015, 2017, 2024 by Stephen A. Davis

Published by Kudu Publishing

All rights reserved. No portion of this book may be reproduced, stored in a retrieval system, or transmitted in any form or by any means—electronic, mechanical, photocopy, recording, scanning, or other—except for brief quotations in critical reviews or articles, without prior written permission of the author.

Unless otherwise noted, Scripture quotations are taken from the New King James Version®. Copyright © 1982 by Thomas Nelson. Used by permission. All rights reserved. | Scripture quotations marked KJV are taken from the King James Version of the Bible. Public domain. | Scripture quotations marked NIV are taken from the Holy Bible, New International Version®, NIV®. Copyright © 1973, 1978, 1984, 2011 by Biblica, Inc.™ Used by permission of Zondervan. All rights reserved worldwide. www.zondervan.com. The "NIV" and "New International Version" are trademarks registered in the United States Patent and Trademark Office by Biblica, Inc.™ | Scripture quotations marked NKJV are taken from the New King James Version®. Copyright © 1982 by Thomas Nelson. Used by permission. All rights reserved. | Scripture quotations marked TLB are taken from The Living Bible copyright © 1971 by Tyndale House Foundation. Used by permission of Tyndale House Publishers Inc., Carol Stream, Illinois 60188. All rights reserved. The Living Bible, TLB, and The Living Bible logo are registered trademarks of Tyndale House Publishers. | Scripture quotations marked NLT are taken from the Holy Bible, New Living Translation, copyright © 1996, 2004, 2015 by Tyndale House Foundation. Used by permission of Tyndale House Publishers, Inc., Carol Stream, Illinois 60188. All rights reserved. | Scripture quotations marked MSG are taken from THE MESSAGE, copyright © 1993, 1994, 1995, 1996, 2000, 2001, 2002 by Eugene H. Peterson. Used by permission of NavPress. All rights reserved. Represented by Tyndale House Publishers, Inc. | Scripture quotations marked NLV are taken from the *New Life Version*, copyright © 1969 and 2003. Used by permission of Barbour Publishing, Inc., Uhrichsville, Ohio 44683. All rights reserved.

For foreign and subsidiary rights, contact the author.

Cover design by Ebbony E. Doty
Cover Photo by Danny Kang Austin

ISBN: 978-1-962401-38-8   1 2 3 4 5 6 7 8 9 10

Printed in the United States of America

WORDS TO INSPIRE YOU TO DREAM

STEPHEN A. DAVIS

HAPPY NEW YEAR!

Psalm 115:14-15 (KJV):
The LORD shall increase you more and more, you and your children. Ye are blessed of the LORD which made heaven and earth.

* * *

GO GET YOUR BLESSING!

IIIIIIIIIIIIIIIIIIIIIIIIIIIIIIIIIIIIIIIIIIIIIIIIIIIIIIIIIIIIIIIIIIIIIIIIIIIIIII

Everything is in place for your journey this year. GO GET YOUR BLESSING!

IIIIIIIIIIIIIIIIIIIIIIIIIIIIIIIIIIIIIIIIIIIIIIIIIIIIIIIIIIIIIIIIIIIIIIIIIIIIIII

Proverbs 10:22:
The blessing of the LORD makes one rich, And He adds no sorrow with it.

NOTES:

OPPORTUNITIES

Your opportunities to succeed are growing, while obstacles are vanishing.

Ephesians 5:15-16 (NIV):
Be very careful, then, how you live—not as unwise but as wise, making the most of every opportunity, because the days are evil.

* * *

RISE UP!

My greatest joy is not to be on top but to help others rise from the bottom.

Philippians 2:4:
Let each of you look out not only for his own interests, but also for the interests of others.

NOTES:

HURDLES?

Life's problems wouldn't be called "hurdles" if there wasn't a way to get over them.

Psalm 34:6:
This poor man cried out, and the LORD heard him, and saved him out of all his troubles.

* * *

CHANGE

Don't be afraid to change what doesn't work; it may be the change that makes life great!

2 Corinthians 5:17 (TLB):
When someone becomes a Christian, he becomes a brand new person inside. He is not the same anymore. A new life has begun!

NOTES:

GREATNESS

If your life were a book, how great would the ending be? Make life GREAT!

Matthew 23:11 (TLB):
"The more lowly your service to others, the greater you are. To be the greatest, be a servant."

* * *

STRETCH

The reason you're being stretched . . .
God wants to get more into you.

Hebrews 11:6:
But without faith it is impossible to please Him, for he who comes to God must believe that He is, and that He is a rewarder of those who diligently seek Him.

NOTES:

DESTINY

The closer you get to your destiny, the more you will appreciate the things you have learned along the way.

Job 8:7:
Though your beginning was small, yet your latter end would increase abundantly.

* * *

AGREE

United we stand, divided we fall. Your agreement will keep your team standing.

Amos 3:3 (NIV):
Do two walk together unless they have agreed to do so?

NOTES:

WORDS

Words can sustain you where you are or move you forward based on the way you use them.

Proverbs 18:21 (MSG):
Words kill, words give life; they are either poison or fruit—you choose.

* * *

DON'T BE SELFISH

Reminder: What you make happen for others God will make happen for you.

1 Peter 4:10 (NIV):
Each one should use whatever gift you have received to serve others, as faithful stewards of God's grace in its various forms.

NOTES:

THE DREAM

When your dream becomes big enough, others will enjoy its reality. Dr. King's DREAM is now a REALITY.

Romans 12:21:
Do not be overcome by evil, but overcome evil with good.

* * *

GREAT THINKING!

The course of your day can be traced back to the influence of your thoughts: Great thinking produces a great day.

Proverbs 23:7a:
For as he thinks in his heart, so is he . . .

NOTES:

ABOVE ONLY

Water underground always finds its way to the surface. You are greater than water; find your way to the top.

1 Peter 2:9 (NIV):
But you are a chosen people, a royal priesthood, a holy nation, God's special possession, that you may declare the praises of him who called you out of darkness into his wonderful light.

* * *

"The enemy is illegal in your life! Cast him out in the name of Jesus!" (Long, 2014)

NOTES:

GET RID OF THE OLD

When the old thing doesn't work, doing something new is not an option.

Galatians 6:15 (NIV):
Neither circumcision nor uncircumcision means anything; what counts is the new creation.

* * *

STRENGTH

Are you strong? I'm STRONG if you're STRONG!

Ecclesiastes 4:12:
Though one may be overpowered by another, two can withstand him. And a threefold cord is not quickly broken.

NOTES:

COMPLETION

Whatever God starts He completes. You are one of His projects, and He will complete you.

Philippians 1:6:
Being confident of this very thing, that He who has begun a good work in you will complete it until the day of Jesus Christ.

* * *

THROUGH THE STORM

Some storms we don't have time to prepare for, but we can find a way to make it through them.

Psalm 121:1-2 (NIV):
I lift up my eyes to the mountains—where does my help come from? My help comes from the LORD, the Maker of heaven and earth.

NOTES:

FOLLOW ME

God is taking you to some great places; take time to see whom you are going to take with you.

Mark 10:21:
Then Jesus, looking at him, loved him, and said to him, "One thing you lack: Go your way, sell whatever you have and give to the poor, and you will have treasure in heaven; and come, take up the cross, and follow Me."

* * *

A BETTER NORMAL

We can say things are getting back to normal, but I say create a new normal, better than the old.

Proverbs 16:16:
How much better to get wisdom than gold! And to get understanding is to be chosen rather than silver.

NOTES:

ARE YOU GLOWING?

Don't let the darkness scare you. Light up and watch darkness flee from you.

Matthew 5:14 (TLB):
You are the world's light—a city on a hill, glowing in the night for all to see.

* * *

SOMETHING GOOD

It's exciting to start something good. Now you're ready to see how it feels to finish something good.

1 Timothy 6:12 (NIV):
Fight the good fight of the faith. Take hold of the eternal life to which you were called when you made your good confession in the presence of many witnesses.

NOTES:

WISDOM

When you have been wise with what's considered less, Heaven will open to send its best.

Proverbs 2:6:
For the LORD gives wisdom; from His mouth come knowledge and understanding;

* * *

CLEAR THE FOG

Things can look foggy when your windows are dirty. Clean those windows and let the sunshine in!

Proverbs 15:30:
The light of the eyes rejoices the heart, and a good report makes the bones healthy.

NOTES:

FEAR OR FAITH

The weather forecast of the past caused us to respond in fear. The forecast for blessing causes us to respond in faith.

2 Timothy 1:7:
For God has not given us a spirit of fear, but of power and of love and of a sound mind.

* * *

STABILITY

Faith is the stability that a shaky life is looking for.

Hebrews 11:1 (NIV):
Now faith is confidence in what we hope for and assurance about what we do not see.

NOTES:

YOU'RE LEGAL

Faith has made you legal to exceed
the generations before you.

Hebrews 12:1:
Therefore we also, since we are surrounded by so great a cloud of witnesses, let us lay aside every weight, and the sin which so easily ensnares us, and let us run with endurance the race that is set before us.

* * *

THE POSSIBLE DREAM

Faith does not allow your dream
to die; it ensures its reality.

Ephesians 3:20:
Now to Him who is able to do exceedingly abundantly above all that we ask or think, according to the power that works in us.

NOTES:

DO YOU HEAR ME NOW?

It's Already Done! Faith comes by HEARING! You heard it, now believe it.

Romans 10:17:
So then faith comes by hearing, and hearing by the word of God.

* * *

TODAY

Today is important. Do not waste a minute of it; make the best of your day!

Matthew 6:33-34 (NIV):
But seek first his kingdom and his righteousness, and all these things will be given to you as well. Therefore do not worry about tomorrow, for tomorrow will worry about itself. Each day has enough trouble of its own.

NOTES:

ENLARGE YOUR TERRITORY

A person thinking in abundance will accomplish the extraordinary.

1 Chronicles 4:10 (NIV):
Jabez cried out to the God of Israel, "Oh, that you would bless me and enlarge my territory! Let your hand be with me, and keep me from harm so that I will be free from pain." And God granted his request.

* * *

A GOOD FUTURE

You will never be able to look at your past and understand how good your future is.

Jeremiah 29:11:
For I know the thoughts that I think toward you, says the LORD, thoughts of peace and not of evil, to give you a future and a hope.

NOTES:

TESTIFY

It's easy to measure your strength, just remember what you have walked through in life.

Revelation 12:11:
And they overcame him by the blood of the Lamb and by the word of their testimony, and they did not love their lives to the death.

* * *

YOU QUALIFY

You're about to stand in a room around people you felt you didn't qualify to be with. Do not be surprised!

Proverbs 18:16:
A man's gift makes room for him, and brings him before great men.

NOTES:

YOU'RE NOT DEFEATED

Do not get discouraged about the place you didn't reach; it's too early to call it defeat.

Romans 8:37:
Yet in all these things we are more than conquerors through Him who loved us.

* * *

GOOD THINGS

Good things are within reach. So make sure your hands are not filled with other things.

Psalm 103:5 (TLB):
He fills my life with good things! My youth is renewed like the eagle's!

NOTES:

READY YOUR MIND!

READY YOUR MIND! The spirit is taking you for a ride that your mind cannot comprehend.

Romans 12:2 (NIV):
Do not conform to the pattern of this world, but be transformed by the renewing of your mind. Then you will be able to test and approve what God's will is—his good, pleasing and perfect will.

* * *

YOUR DIVINE POTENTIAL

The moment you realize your potential the limits will no longer exist.

1 John 4:4:
You are of God, little children, and have overcome them, because He who is in you is greater than he who is in the world.

NOTES:

PREPARATION

Faith is preparing for a day you
have not experienced before.

2 Corinthians 5:7 (NIV):
For we live by faith, not by sight.

* * *

WHAT'S YOUR GOAL?

Start each day in a goal-oriented way and don't forget, hard work will create a little time to play.

Philippians 3:14 (NIV):
I press on toward the goal to win the prize for which God has called me heavenward in Christ Jesus.

NOTES:

WHAT'S YOUR PURPOSE?

Purpose is so important, that when you find it everything in life will make sense.

Jeremiah 1:5 (TLB):
"I knew you before you were formed within your mother's womb; before you were born I sanctified you and appointed you as my spokesman to the world."

* * *

IT'S POSSIBLE

It's a great time for something amazing to happen in your life, so believe it's possible.

Luke 1:37:
"For with God nothing will be impossible."

NOTES:

LIVE ON TOP

You've lived underneath your situations long enough, now it's time to live on top of them.

Deuteronomy 28:13:
"And the LORD will make you the head and not the tail; you shall be above only, and not be beneath, if you heed the commandments of the LORD your God, which I command you today, and are careful to observe them."

* * *

YOUR MIRACLE IS HERE

This is the moment of TRUTH, so don't believe the LIES of the devil. Your miracle is here!

Acts 19:11-12:
Now God worked unusual miracles by the hands of Paul, so that even handkerchiefs or aprons were brought from his body to the sick, and the diseases left them and the evil spirits went out of them.

NOTES:

DREAM FORWARD

No more thinking back, it's
time to dream forward.

Joel 2:28:
"And it shall come to pass afterward that I will pour out My Spirit on all flesh; your sons and your daughters shall prophesy, your old men shall dream dreams, your young men shall see visions."

* * *

LISTEN

Just because it is quiet does not mean
God's not speaking. Listen a little closer!

John 10:27-28:
"My sheep hear My voice, and I know them, and they follow Me. And I give them eternal life, and they shall never perish; neither shall anyone snatch them out of My hand."

NOTES:

GOOD NEWS

Good news is always available, so you don't have to tolerate bad news.

Acts 8:12:
But when they believed Philip as he preached the things concerning the kingdom of God and the name of Jesus Christ, both men and women were baptized.

* * *

FAITH

Faith makes you tall enough to ride the big rides in life.

Hebrews 11:1:
Now faith is the substance of things hoped for, the evidence of things not seen.

NOTES:

COURAGE

Just when you thought opportunity had passed you by, some soft voice said, "Give it another try!"

Deuteronomy 31:6:
"Be strong and of good courage, do not fear nor be afraid of them; for the LORD your God, He is the One who goes with you. He will not leave you nor forsake you."

* * *

SUCCESS IS REAL

This time you will really achieve success; your days of pretending are over.

Proverbs 16:3:
Commit your works to the LORD, and your thoughts will be established.

NOTES:

THE LORD

It is the fear of The Lord that cancels
fear of any other threat.

Proverbs 1:7:
*The fear of the LORD is the beginning of knowledge,
but fools despise wisdom and instruction.*

* * *

TAKE A STAND

When good people stand for the
right things, others will experience
a life filled with great things.

1 Peter 1:13:
*Therefore gird up the loins of your mind, be sober,
and rest your hope fully upon the grace that is to be
brought to you at the revelation of Jesus Christ.*

NOTES:

REST IN HIM

Sleep is needed to refresh and rest, while too much sleep can set you behind on God's best.

Mark 6:31:
And He said to them, "Come aside by yourselves to a deserted place and rest a while." For there were many coming and going, and they did not even have time to eat.

* * *

CONFIDENCE

Confidence is what you should have when you're receiving your victory by faith.

1 John 5:14-15:
Now this is the confidence that we have in Him, that if we ask anything according to His will, He hears us. And if we know that He hears us, whatever we ask, we know that we have the petitions that we have asked of Him.

NOTES:

ONE ACCORD

We were not created to think alike
but to put our thoughts together.

Philippians 2:2:
... *fulfill my joy by being like-minded, having the same love, being of one accord, of one mind.*

* * *

SEED TIME

If God's word is seed, it is time to make
sure your field [heart] is full.

2 Corinthians 9:10:
Now may He who supplies seed to the sower, and bread for food, supply and multiply the seed you have sown and increase the fruits of your righteousness....

NOTES:

SUPPORT SOMEONE

Today you can make a difference by doing something good or supporting someone doing good.

1 Thessalonians 5:11:
Therefore comfort each other and edify one another, just as you also are doing.

* * *

IT'S WORKING FOR YOU

The odds don't mean you're losing. God seems to work more effectively when the odds are against you.

Romans 8:28:
And we know that all things work together for good to those who love God, to those who are the called according to His purpose.

NOTES:

HE CREATED YOU

No one will ever be able to compete with the real you. So stay real to who you are.

Genesis 1:27:
So God created man in His own image; in the image of God He created him; male and female He created them.

* * *

BELIEVE IT!

You can see it! You can believe it! You can have it!

Matthew 21:22:
"And whatever things you ask in prayer, believing, you will receive."

NOTES:

TIME FOR GROWTH

God has created you to grow.
So get ready for expansion.

1 Corinthians 2:6 (MSG):
We, of course, have plenty of wisdom to pass on to you once you get your feet on firm spiritual ground, but it's not popular wisdom, the fashionable wisdom of high-priced experts that will be out-of-date in a year or so.

* * *

RESOURCES COME!

Faith can bring an ongoing supply of resources for a believer. NO MORE SHORTAGE!

Philippians 4:19:
And my God shall supply all your need according to His riches in glory by Christ Jesus.

NOTES:

GET YOUR MIRACLE!

Miracles are a place in God, not an event.
You're in that place . . . Get your miracle!

John 4:48:
Then Jesus said to him, "Unless you people see signs and wonders, you will by no means believe."

* * *

THE POTTER AND THE CLAY

Because God refers to you as clay,
know that He is making a better you today.
Don't get discouraged in any way;
the way you are is not how you'll stay.

Isaiah 64:8:
But now, O LORD, You are our Father; We are the clay, and You our potter; And all we are the work of Your hand.

NOTES:

RISE UP!

Your consistency to stand causes
others to rise from sitting.

John 5:8:
Jesus said to him, "Rise, take up your bed and walk."

* * *

SUPERNATURAL

Resistance is an announcement that
you have moved beyond average.

Luke 10:9:
"And heal the sick there, and say to them, 'The kingdom of God has come near to you.'"

NOTES:

ENCOURAGE YOURSELF

There are compliments we wait to hear from others. Shorten your wait and compliment yourself.

Philippians 4:13:
I can do all things through Christ who strengthens me.

* * *

POWER IN AGREEMENT

Just adding my agreement with you today, that your dream becomes a reality!

Amos 3:3:
Can two walk together, unless they are agreed?

NOTES:

NO WORRIES

Never worry about losing your place to someone else, you were born for this place.

Philippians 4:6-7:
Be anxious for nothing, but in everything by prayer and supplication, with thanksgiving, let your requests be made known to God; and the peace of God, which surpasses all understanding, will guard your hearts and minds through Christ Jesus.

* * *

YOU WIN!

Life is easier when you've settled on the mountain. The devil now has an uphill battle against you, which means you always win!

Isaiah 54:17:
"No weapon formed against you shall prosper, and every tongue which rises against you in judgment You shall condemn. This is the heritage of the servants of the LORD, and their righteousness is from Me," says the LORD.

NOTES:

THIS IS THE DAY

Today will be better than yesterday even if yesterday was a good day. Every day is great when you are alive!

Psalm 118:24:
This is the day the LORD has made; we will rejoice and be glad in it.

* * *

GREATNESS IN PURPOSE

Just when you think you've given your all, God reminds you of the greatness of your call.

John 14:12:
"Most assuredly, I say to you, he who believes in Me, the works that I do he will do also; and greater works than these he will do, because I go to My Father."

NOTES:

JUST STAND

When you're not sure what to do, take a stand and see your situation all the way through.

Psalm 46:10:
Be still, and know that I am God; I will be exalted among the nations, I will be exalted in the earth!

* * *

DESTINED TO BE

We know some good things are destined for us. I am convinced it's now.

Jeremiah 29:11:
For I know the thoughts that I think toward you, says the LORD, thoughts of peace and not of evil, to give you a future and a hope.

NOTES:

A GREAT FUTURE

It's always easier to turn when you're in motion. Make the turn toward your great future.

3 John 1:2 (MSG):
How truly I love you! We're the best of friends, and I pray for good fortune in everything you do, and for your good health—that your everyday affairs prosper, as well as your soul!

* * *

IS AVAILABLE

Help is always available when the people around you are unselfish. Choose your friends well; you may need them.

Ephesians 2:21:
In whom the whole building, being fitted together, grows into a holy temple in the Lord.

NOTES:

MAKE A DIFFERENCE

Making a difference begins with recognizing a need. You can make a difference.

Proverbs 22:9:
He who has a generous eye will be blessed, for he gives of his bread to the poor.

* * *

FREEDOM

Freedom is available and bondage has been removed from the life of the believer. Live free!

Galatians 5:13 (MSG):
It is absolutely clear that God has called you to a free life. Just make sure that you don't use this freedom as an excuse to do whatever you want to do and destroy your freedom. Rather, use your freedom to serve one another in love; that's how freedom grows.

NOTES:

ASK

In the past I spent lots of time wondering what people close to me were thinking, now I just ask them. Asking questions saves a lot of time.

Matthew 7:7-8:
"Ask, and it will be given to you; seek, and you will find; knock, and it will be opened to you. For everyone who asks receives, and he who seeks finds, and to him who knocks it will be opened."

* * *

MOUNT UP LIKE EAGLES!

In this season aviation laws are important because you're flying, not walking.
Mount up with wings like eagles!

Isaiah 40:31:
But those who wait on the LORD Shall renew their strength; they shall mount up with wings like eagles, they shall run and not be weary, they shall walk and not faint.

NOTES:

PENTECOST

If you are reading this statement, destruction (storm) PASSED OVER. Now look forward to Pentecost.

Acts 2:1-4:

When the Day of Pentecost had fully come, they were all with one accord in one place. And suddenly there came a sound from heaven, as of a rushing mighty wind, and it filled the whole house where they were sitting. Then there appeared to them divided tongues, as of fire, and one sat upon each of them. And they were all filled with the Holy Spirit and began to speak with other tongues, as the Spirit gave them utterance.

* * *

NOTES:

OVERFLOW

Never stop pouring when your container is full. Someone close needs your overflow.

Joel 2:24:
The threshing floors shall be full of wheat, And the vats shall overflow with new wine and oil.

* * *

THE NATIONS!

May 1st—It's National Day of Prayer! Praying for our nation today!

Psalm 33:12:
Blessed is the nation whose God is the LORD, The people He has chosen as His own inheritance.

NOTES:

GLORY

Get ready to give God the glory because He's giving you an incredible life story.

Exodus 33:18:
And he said, "Please, show me Your glory."

* * *

HE IS PLEASED!

Do your best in all you do, this insures that God is pleased with you.

Matthew 3:17:
And suddenly a voice came from heaven, saying, "This is My beloved Son, in whom I am well pleased."

* * *

"Distraction is the enemy of greatness . . . STAY FOCUSED!" (Long, 2014)

NOTES:

NEW LIFE!

What you hear can be powerful but what you experience is life changing. Your Life Has Changed!

2 Corinthians 5:17:
Therefore, if anyone is in Christ, he is a new creation; old things have passed away; behold, all things have become new.

* * *

SUCCESS IS YOURS

When confusion is dispelled success is imminent for the believer.

Psalm 37:4:
Delight yourself also in the LORD, And He shall give you the desires of your heart.

NOTES:

HE MADE THE WAY

Jesus came to make things right; keep believing and your life will be out of sight!

John 14:6:
Jesus said to him, "I am the way, the truth, and the life. No one comes to the Father except through Me."

* * *

TRUTH

Things will get better. We know that's true . . . your individual faith can cause it to get better for you.

Psalm 16:8:
I have set the LORD always before me; Because He is at my right hand I shall not be moved.

NOTES:

HE BLOCKED IT

Everything you felt taken away was just blocking the place for what God is sending.

Isaiah 57:14:
And one shall say, "Heap it up! Heap it up! Prepare the way, Take the stumbling block out of the way of My people."

* * *

HUMBLE SERVANT!

If you're in the game of life, you can win in the final moment by serving Jesus Christ.

John 12:26:
"If anyone serves Me, let him follow Me; and where I am, there My servant will be also. If anyone serves Me, him My Father will honor."

NOTES:

"God says, 'Stir up the gift that I have placed within you and watch as DOORS are unlocked to give you access to your destiny and purpose.'" (Long, 2014)

* * *

GET AHEAD

If being behind has gotten boring,
it is time to get ahead.

Proverbs 21:5 (MSG):
*Careful planning puts you ahead in the long run;
hurry and scurry puts you further behind.*

NOTES:

BE ENCOURAGED!

Treat encouragement as a "friend" you always want around. You need it every day.

John 15:15:
"No longer do I call you servants, for a servant does not know what his master is doing; but I have called you friends, for all things that I heard from My Father I have made known to you."

* * *

NEVER STOP LEARNING

What I've learned brought me to where I am; learning more will help me get to where I'm going.

2 Timothy 2:15 (KJV):
Study to shew thyself approved unto God, a workman that needeth not to be ashamed, rightly dividing the word of truth.

NOTES:

WALK THROUGH IT

Never stop believing in your dream while you're walking through your process.

Deuteronomy 5:33:
You shall walk in all the ways which the LORD your God has commanded you, that you may live and that it may be well with you, and that you may prolong your days in the land which you shall possess.

* * *

SHOUT!

Can you believe that your wait is over? SHOUT NOW!

Psalm 47:1 (KJV):
O clap your hands, all ye people; shout unto God with the voice of triumph.

NOTES:

SEASONS CHANGE

This season of opportunity will make up for all the opportunities you may have missed.

Daniel 2:21 (NIV):
He changes times and seasons; he deposes kings and raises up others. He gives wisdom to the wise and knowledge to the discerning.

* * *

TRUE SACRIFICE

End of May—Happy Memorial Day! Remembering all who sacrificed so much!

John 3:16:
"For God so loved the world that He gave His only begotten Son, that whoever believes in Him should not perish but have everlasting life."

NOTES:

HIS PRESENCE

God is never far away from you. You're just more aware of Him at certain times than others.

Psalm 73:23-24 (NIV):
Yet I am always with you; you hold me by my right hand. You guide me with your counsel, and afterward you will take me into glory.

* * *

RELATIONSHIPS

Relationships are like elevators; they take you either up or down.

Hebrews 10:25:
Not forsaking the assembling of ourselves together, as is the manner of some, but exhorting one another, and so much the more as you see the Day approaching.

NOTES:

BE READY!

Everything that seemed slow in arriving has just been accelerated. BE READY!

1 Peter 3:15:
But sanctify the Lord God in your hearts, and always be ready to give a defense to everyone who asks you a reason for the hope that is in you, with meekness and fear;

* * *

THINK POSITIVE!

A positive mind is a great weapon against worry and depression. Think Positive!

Philippians 4:8:
Finally, brethren, whatever things are true, whatever things are noble, whatever things are just, whatever things are pure, whatever things are lovely, whatever things are of good report, if there is any virtue and if there is anything praiseworthy—meditate on these things.

NOTES:

SPEAK LIFE!

Speaking positive words today!

Proverbs 18:21:
Death and life are in the power of the tongue, and those who love it will eat its fruit.

* * *

LET GO!

Practice learning to let go and as you do, God will bless beyond what you know.

Isaiah 43:18-19 (NIV):
"Forget the former things; do not dwell on the past. See, I am doing a new thing! Now it springs up; do you not perceive it?"

NOTES:

IT'S DONE!

The prophetic word to you today is "IT'S DONE!"

Revelation 21:6 (NIV):
He said to me: "It is done. I am the Alpha and the Omega, the Beginning and the End. To the thirsty I will give water without cost from the spring of the water of life."

* * *

CELEBRATE

Today is a day of celebration: Victory is yours!

1 Corinthians 15:57:
57 But thanks be to God, who gives us the victory through our Lord Jesus Christ.

NOTES:

NO OPTION!

When God has gone before you, Satan has no option but to get behind you.

Matthew 16:23:
But He turned and said to Peter, "Get behind Me, Satan! You are an offense to Me, for you are not mindful of the things of God, but the things of men."

* * *

"Your hardest times often lead to the greatest moments of your life. Keep the faith .it will all be worth it in the end." (Long, 2014)

NOTES:

YOU ARE IMPORTANT

You're about to find out how important you are to the people around you.

Psalm 8:4-5:
What is man that You are mindful of him, And the son of man that You visit him? For You have made him a little lower than the angels, and You have crowned him with glory and honor.

* * *

GOOD DAYS

Your good days are announcing to your bad days that the seasons have changed. Good days will rule this season.

Matthew 6:33 (NIV):
But seek first his kingdom and his righteousness, and all these things will be given to you as well.

NOTES:

LOOK FORWARD!

You have too much to look forward
to, so stop looking back!

Proverbs 3:5-6:
*Trust in the LORD with all your heart, and lean
not on your own understanding; in all your ways
acknowledge Him, and He shall direct your paths.*

* * *

REFUSE TO QUIT

Big things happen when little
people refuse to quit.

2 Timothy 3:14:
*But you must continue in the things which you
have learned and been assured of, knowing
from whom you have learned them,*

NOTES:

GOD'S FAVOR

It's okay when religious minds challenge you, because God has favored you.

Luke 2:52:
And Jesus increased in wisdom and stature, and in favor with God and men.

* * *

"Today's thought: In just a few words, someone can change your perspective that in turn can change your life!" (Long, 2014)

* * *

LOVE YOUR NEIGHBOR

How you love those around you is a reflection of how much you love yourself. Love your neighbor as yourself.

Mark 12:31:
"And the second, like it, is this: 'You shall love your neighbor as yourself.'"

NOTES:

ENOJOY THE BLESSING

It's a wonderful thing when you hear great times are for now; it is better when you know how to enjoy them.

Ecclesiastes 5:19:
As for every man to whom God has given riches and wealth, and given him power to eat of it, to receive his heritage and rejoice in his labor—this is the gift of God.

* * *

A LAP AHEAD

Just when you thought you were a few feet behind, you quickly realized you were about to be a lap ahead.

1 Corinthians 9:24:
Do you not know that those who run in a race all run, but one receives the prize? Run in such a way that you may obtain it.

NOTES:

TOMORROW

Yesterday's problems are too far behind
to have any effect on your tomorrow.

Romans 8:38-39:
For I am persuaded that neither death nor0 life, nor angels nor principalities nor powers, nor things present nor things to come, nor height nor depth, nor any other created thing, shall be able to separate us from the love of God which is in Christ Jesus our Lord.

* * *

AWAITED TIME!

The long-awaited time of God's
favor is here. Love you!

Isaiah 49:8 (NIV):
This is what the LORD says: "In the time of my favor I will answer you, and in the day of salvation I will help you; I will keep you and will make you to be a covenant for the people, to restore the land and to reassign its desolate inheritances."

NOTES:

GREAT LIFE!

You can forget some things in life but never forget to live a great life.

Deuteronomy 30:19-20:
"I call heaven and earth as witnesses today against you, that I have set before you life and death, blessing and cursing; therefore choose life, that both you and your descendants may live; that you may love the LORD your God, that you may obey His voice, and that you may cling to Him, for He is your life and the length of your days; and that you may dwell in the land which the LORD swore to your fathers, to Abraham, Isaac, and Jacob, to give them."

* * *

NOTES:

RECEIVE

This blessing is so easy to receive; you will have to work hard to miss it.

John 15:7 (NIV):
If you remain in me and my words remain in you, ask whatever you wish, and it will be done for you.

* * *

"There is a fresh move of My [God's] Spirit being released NOW! Lift your hands now and begin to receive the NEW! New life is upon you!" (Long, 2014)

NOTES:

GREAT VICTORY!

This week is the beginning of another week of great victory.

Joshua 10:8 (KJV):
And the LORD said unto Joshua, Fear them not: for I have delivered them into thine hand; there shall not a man of them stand before thee.

* * *

PRAY WITHOUT CEASING

If PRAYER makes you fly high, PRAY more and you'll never CRASH!

1 Thessalonians 5:17 (KJV):
Pray without ceasing.

NOTES:

HARD TIMES DON'T LAST!

What's ahead of you will one day be behind you, so know that hard times don't last always.

Romans 8:18 (NIV):
I consider that our present sufferings are not worth comparing with the glory that will be revealed in us.

* * *

TRIAL TO TRIUMPH!

It's too late to stop you now; your trial did not triumph over you.

Deuteronomy 7:19:
The great trials which your eyes saw, the signs and the wonders, the mighty hand and the outstretched arm, by which the LORD your God brought you out. So shall the LORD your God do to all the peoples of whom you are afraid.

NOTES:

DREAM

When you've gone very far, seen many things,
just remember, it all started with a dream.

Acts 2:17 (AMP):
"And it shall come to pass in the last days," says God, "that I will pour out my spirit upon all mankind; and your sons and your daughters shall prophesy, and your young men shall see [divinely prompted] visions, and your old men shall dream [divinely prompted] dreams."

* * *

A GUARANTEED HIGH

If going low occurs before you go high,
you're on your way to a really high place!

Matthew 23:12:
"And whoever exalts himself will be humbled, and he who humbles himself will be exalted."

NOTES:

MIRACLES

The devil may have created a mess in some areas of your life, but Jesus is doing miracles in every area of your life.

John 10:10:
"The thief does not come except to steal, and to kill, and to destroy. I have come that they may have life, and that they may have it more abundantly."

* * *

TAKING AUTHORITY

We take authority over this day, expecting it to produce in a favorable way!

Luke 10:19:
"Behold, I give you the authority to trample on serpents and scorpions, and over all the power of the enemy, and nothing shall by any means hurt you."

NOTES:

YOUR FAVORABLE SEASON!

What God has started He will finish and you're His masterpiece. Your favorable season is HERE!

Proverbs 3:5-6:
Trust in the Lord with all your heart, and lean not on your own understanding; in all your ways acknowledge Him, and He shall direct your paths.

* * *

NO FEAR

Faith is now ruling in your life;
fear has to submit and flee.

2 Timothy 1:7:
For God has not given us a spirit of fear, but of power and of love and of a sound mind.

NOTES:

GOOD COMING YOUR WAY

So much good is coming your way, that you won't be able to remember the bad things of yesterday.

Psalm 34:8:
*Oh, taste and see that the LORD is good;
Blessed is the man who trusts in Him!*

* * *

ONE DAY

In one day your life can change for the better. Are you ready?

2 Peter 3:8:
But, beloved, do not forget this one thing, that with the Lord one day is as a thousand years, and a thousand years as one day.

NOTES:

NEW LIFE

Faith has created a life for you that
fear said could never exist.

James 2:26:
*For as the body without the spirit is dead,
so faith without works is dead also.*

* * *

VICTORIOUS!

Every trial is an opportunity to gain
victory. You are VICTORIOUS!

1 Corinthians 15:57:
*But thanks be to God, who gives us the
victory through our Lord Jesus Christ.*

NOTES:

JUST RECEIVE

God is sending someone to show you kindness, JUST RECEIVE IT!

Matthew 7:8:
"For everyone who asks receives, and he who seeks finds, and to him who knocks it will be opened."

* * *

GIVE

Encouragement is not illegal, so give and receive as much as possible.

1 Thessalonians 5:11:
Therefore comfort each other and edify one another, just as you also are doing.

NOTES:

WISDOM

Wisdom will bring an early release
from a challenging season.

James 1:5:
If any of you lacks wisdom, let him ask of God, who gives to all liberally and without reproach, and it will be given to him.

* * *

"The Lord says, 'I will not allow the weapons formed against you to prosper! My vengeance is upon all that which tries to destroy your destiny.'" (Long, 2014)

NOTES:

YOU'RE DIFFERENT

Making a difference starts when you embrace the fact that you are different.

1 Peter 2:9 (TLB):
But you are not like that, for you have been chosen by God himself—you are priests of the King, you are holy and pure, you are God's very own—all this so that you may show to others how God called you out of the darkness into his wonderful light.

* * *

FAITH

Faith can restore the life you had or build the life you would like to have.

Matthew 17:20:
So Jesus said to them, "Because of your unbelief; for assuredly, I say to you, if you have faith as a mustard seed, you will say to this mountain, 'Move from here to there,' and it will move; and nothing will be impossible for you . . . ."

NOTES:

DIFFICULTY

It seems difficult for a moment,
but it will be worth it all.

Luke 6:18 (NLT):
They had come to hear him and to be healed of their diseases; and those troubled by evil spirits were healed.

* * *

SUCCESS ONLY

Faith is a weapon that causes failure
to surrender to success.

James 2:20:
But do you want to know, O foolish man, that faith without works is dead?

NOTES:

|||||||||||||||||||||||||||||||||||||||||||||||||||||||||||||||||||||||||||||

"The Lord says, 'I AM pouring out My strength upon you to erase your areas of weakness! I have assigned grace to empower you to do all things!'" (Long, 2014)

|||||||||||||||||||||||||||||||||||||||||||||||||||||||||||||||||||||||||||||

* * *

IT'S YOUR TIME!

Ecclesiastes 9:11 (NLT):
I have observed something else under the sun. The fastest runner doesn't always win the race, and the strongest warrior doesn't always win the battle. The wise sometimes go hungry, and the skillful are not necessarily wealthy. And those who are educated don't always lead successful lives. It is all decided by chance, by being in the right place at the right time.

NOTES:

BELIEVE & RECEIVE

Believe it and receive it! It's yours!

Mark 11:24:
"Therefore I say to you, whatever things you ask when you pray, believe that you receive them, and you will have them."

* * *

TIME FOR INCREASE!

It is time to possess; so increase your kingdom inventory.

Proverbs 1:5:
A wise man will hear and increase learning, and a man of understanding will attain wise counsel,

NOTES:

"The Lord says, 'I AM releasing new favor and new glory upon you! Behold, I AM making all things new, for this is a season of new beginnings!'" (Long, 2014)

* * *

STRENGTH FOR BATTLE

Your uphill battle has made you a mountaintop success.

Psalm 18:39 (NIV):
You armed me with strength for battle; you humbled my adversaries before me.

* * *

"The Lord says, 'I AM depositing a new level of My grace upon your life to make you sufficient in all areas! Draw from Me and BREAK THROUGH!'" (Long, 2014)

NOTES:

THE BATTLE IS THE LORD'S!

2 Chronicles 20:15:
And he said, "Listen, all you of Judah and you inhabitants of Jerusalem, and you, King Jehoshaphat! Thus says the LORD to you: 'Do not be afraid nor dismayed because of this great multitude, for the battle is not yours, but God's.'"

* * *

WALK BY FAITH

The walk of faith will always get you to your destination.

2 Corinthians 5:7:
For we walk by faith, not by sight.

NOTES:

LIVE BY FAITH

Procrastination is terrified of people who live by faith.

Ephesians 2:8:
For by grace you have been saved through faith, and that not of yourselves; it is the gift of God,

* * *

EXPAND YOUR DREAM

Faith in your team brings expansion to your dream.

Proverbs 28:20:
A faithful man will abound with blessings, but he who hastens to be rich will not go unpunished.

NOTES:

YOU'RE UNSTOPPABLE

Hell cannot stop your SET TIME!

Psalm 102:13:
You will arise and have mercy on Zion; for the time to favor her, yes, the set time, has come.

* * *

THE GOOD THINGS

No good thing will be withheld from you.

Proverbs 13:21 (NIV):
Trouble pursues the sinner, but the righteous are rewarded with good things.

NOTES:

STRAIGHT AHEAD

The road you travel determines the destiny you reach. Stay on the right road!

Proverbs 4:25-27:
Let your eyes look straight ahead, and your eyelids look right before you. Ponder the path of your feet, and let all your ways be established. Do not turn to the right or the left; remove your foot from evil.

* * *

"The Lord says, 'Don't be discouraged or afraid! My purpose for you will ALWAYS stand and prevail! As I spoke it, so shall it come to pass!'" (Long, 2014)

NOTES:

THE FUTURE

Don't drown in your past when you can swim in your future.

Proverbs 23:18 (NIV):
There is surely a future hope for you, and your hope will not be cut off.

* * *

"Today's thought: 'If you see it in the Spirit, you can possess it in the natural.'" (Long, 2014)

* * *

TRUTH OVER LIES

Believe God's truth and shatter Satan's lies.

John 8:31-32:
Then Jesus said to those Jews who believed Him, "If you abide in My word, you are My disciples indeed. And you shall know the truth, and the truth shall make you free."

NOTES:

NEW DIMENSIONS

Never mistake a new dimension as starting over. Every dimension starts at zero.

John 3:3:
Jesus answered and said to him, "Most assuredly, I say to you, unless one is born again, he cannot see the kingdom of God."

* * *

KEEP MOVING!

There is NO stopping you now,
you're on the move!

Philippians 4:13:
I can do all things through Christ who strengthens me.

NOTES:

VICTORY

The good fight of faith is the fight
that claims many victories.

1 Corinthians 15:57:
*But thanks be to God, who gives us the
victory through our Lord Jesus Christ.*

* * *

FAITH THAT LIFTS

Faith has the ability to recover
from the lowest place.

Psalm 24:7:
*Lift up your heads, O you gates! And be lifted up, you
everlasting doors! And the King of glory shall come in.*

NOTES:

SPEAK IT

You will only experience the power of God's word when you speak it.

Mark 11:23:
"For assuredly, I say to you, whoever says to this mountain, 'Be removed and be cast into the sea,' and does not doubt in his heart, but believes that those things he says will be done, he will have whatever he says."

* * *

"The Lord says, 'I AM anointing and opening your eyes to see the harvest that's surrounding you! Now RISE UP and GO FORTH! The harvest is here.'" (Long, 2014)

NOTES:

VICTORY IS MINE!

Tell Satan to get behind you because today, VICTORY is yours!

1 John 5:4 (NLT):
For every child of God defeats this evil world, and we achieve this victory through our faith.

* * *

GLORY

The Glory of God is filling the earth NOW!

Psalm 19:1 (NIV):
The heavens declare the glory of God; the skies proclaim the work of his hands.

NOTES:

IF GOD IS FOR YOU?

Whatever you're facing, God is also fighting.

Romans 8:31:
What then shall we say to these things? If God is for us, who can be against us?

* * *

LEARN AND GROW

Never stop learning, and you will never stop growing.

Proverbs 9:9 (NLV):
Give teaching to a wise man and he will be even wiser. Teach a man who is right and good, and he will grow in learning.

* * *

"Don't let yesterday take up [use] too much of today."
(Rogers as quoted by Long, 2014)

NOTES:

"The Lord says, 'Do not cast away your confidence! STAND BOLDLY in the face of all adversity, and I WILL deliver you and elevate you to the top.'" (Long, 2014)

* * *

THE PRECIOUS SEED

Your PRECIOUS SEED has released a BLESSING you do not have room to receive.

Matthew 13:8 (NIV):
Still other seed fell on good soil, where it produced a crop—a hundred, sixty or thirty times what was sown.

NOTES:

THE PRECIOUS!

When you give what is PRECIOUS,
God will send what is GLORIOUS!

Matthew 6:21:
For where your treasure is, there your heart will be also.

* * *

CLOSER

You're closer to where you're going
than where you've been.

Psalm 25:3:
Indeed, let no one who waits on You be ashamed; let those be ashamed who deal treacherously without cause.

NOTES:

BE A BLESSING

It's a great time to be BLESSED
and to be a BLESSING!

Genesis 12:2:
I will make you a great nation; I will bless you and make your name great; and you shall be a blessing.

* * *

"If you saw the size of the blessing coming, you would understand the magnitude of the battle you are fighting." (Long, 2014)

NOTES:

YOUR BEST DAY

Everyday can be the best day of
your life if you believe it.

Matthew 8:13:
Then Jesus said to the centurion, "Go your way; and as you have believed, so let it be done for you." And his servant was healed that same hour.

* * *

GOT A WORD?

When you have a word for each day,
battles are won right away.

Matthew 7:24:
"Therefore whoever hears these sayings of Mine, and does them, I will liken him to a wise man who built his house on the rock:"

NOTES:

MAKING SENSE

God is making all the nonsense
in your life make sense.

Proverbs 1:7 (NIV):
*The fear of the LORD is the beginning of knowledge,
but fools despise wisdom and instruction.*

* * *

ENCOURAGE OTHERS

Make the day great by
encouraging someone else.

Proverbs 11:25 (NIV):
*A generous person will prosper; whoever
refreshes others will be refreshed.*

NOTES:

THE SAINTS ARE WINNING!

We have entered the season of The Lord which means the Saints are winning.

Joshua 1:7 (NIV):
"Be strong and very courageous. Be careful to obey all the law my servant Moses gave you; do not turn from it to the right or to the left, that you may be successful wherever you go."

* * *

IT'S TIME TO WORSHIP

Make your decision: Are you going to WAR or WORSHIP? It's time to WORSHIP!

1 Chronicles 16:29:
Give to the LORD the glory due His name; Bring an offering, and come before Him. Oh, worship the LORD in the beauty of holiness!

NOTES:

BLESSING OF A LIFETIME

In this time of Prayer and Fasting,
we are positioning ourselves for
the blessing of a lifetime.

Isaiah 44:3:
For I will pour water on him who is thirsty, and floods on the dry ground; I will pour My Spirit on your descendants, and My blessing on your offspring;

* * *

UNINTERRUPTED BLESSING

This is the BEGINNING of a
PERPETUAL BLESSING!

Psalm 133:3:
3 It is like the dew of Hermon, descending upon the mountains of Zion; for there the LORD commanded the blessing—Life forevermore.

NOTES:

"People who are crazy enough to think they can change the world are the ones that DO!" —Steve Jobs

* * *

Let's change the world for JESUS." (Long, 2014)

* * *

RECOVER

You're invited into God's season of recovery.

1 Samuel 30:8:
So David inquired of the LORD, saying, "Shall I pursue this troop? Shall I overtake them?" And He answered him, "Pursue, for you shall surely overtake them and without fail recover all."

NOTES:

YOUR SEASON

Keep doing good, for this is your DUE SEASON!

Galatians 6:9:
And let us not grow weary while doing good, for in due season we shall reap if we do not lose heart.

* * *

MIRACLES

Miracles are still for today. Are you looking for a MIRACLE?

Acts 2:22 (NIV):
"Fellow Israelites, listen to this: Jesus of Nazareth was a man accredited by God to you by miracles, wonders and signs, which God did among you through him, as you yourselves know."

NOTES:

MAKE GOD BIGGER

If you always make sure God is bigger than you, you don't have to worry about being defeated!

1 John 4:4:
4 You are of God, little children, and have overcome them, because He who is in you is greater than he who is in the world.

* * *

"When you refuse to address your weakness, you will not discover your strength." (Long, 2014)

* * *

REJOICE!

This is the Day that The Lord has made; I will rejoice and be glad in it.

Philippians 4:4:
Rejoice in the Lord always. Again I will say, rejoice!

NOTES:

FAITH WITH POWER

You use your faith and let God use His power!

2 Thessalonians 1:11:
Therefore we also pray always for you that our God would count you worthy of this calling, and fulfill all the good pleasure of His goodness and the work of faith with power,

* * *

YOU'RE COVERED

God Has You Covered!

Romans 4:7:
"Blessed are those whose lawless deeds are forgiven, and whose sins are covered."

NOTES:

"Why walk in darkness when you have the light?" (Long, 2014)

* * *

"There's an old saying that Noah didn't wait for his ship to come in; he built one! Let's pray and build! It's prayer time, saints!" (Long, 2014)

* * *

JUST DO IT!

Now OR Never! What you do now can BLESS you forever.

Hebrews 11:1:
Now faith is the substance of things hoped for, the evidence of things not seen.

NOTES:

"The Lord says, 'NOW is the time for you to rise up and break through! Your season of waiting has built up your strength! NOW ARISE IN VICTORY!'" (Long, 2014)

* * *

"Your purpose is locked away in your heart so that no one can control your destiny" (Long, 2014)

* * *

OVERCOMER!

You are an overcomer!

1 John 5:4:
For whatever is born of God overcomes the world. And this is the victory that has overcome the world—our faith.

NOTES:

"Today's thought: God's Wisdom is so accurate that He doesn't have a backup plan, because his first plan is always the solution." (Long, 2014)

* * *

"The Lord says, 'I AM renewing your strength for victory! DON'T GIVE UP! Receive a fresh wind of My Spirit and be revived for the future!'" (Long, 2014)

* * *

GOD'S PEACE

God's peace is resting on you today.

Philippians 4:7:
And the peace of God, which surpasses all understanding, will guard your hearts and minds through Christ Jesus.

NOTES:

"The Lord says, 'Mountains will begin to move out of your way when you speak My WORD with faith! Do not allow doubt to stop you! Speak BOLDLY!'" (Long, 2014)

* * *

"FAITH does not make announcements of a future reality; it creates new, present realities. Faith is not futuristic, it is always current...." (Long, 2014)

* * *

IT'S YOUR RIGHT TO VOTE!

It's time to VOTE!

Matthew 5:37:
But let your 'Yes' be 'Yes,' and your 'No,' 'No.' For whatever is more than these is from the evil one.

NOTES:

KEEP LEARNING

What you learn along the way is as important as the destination.

Proverbs 1:5:
A wise man will hear and increase learning, and a man of understanding will attain wise counsel,

* * *

"The Lord says, 'Walls will FALL before you as you release the sound of praise and faith from your lips! Praise will release promised victory!'" (Long, 2014)

NOTES:

PUBLIC VICTORY

It is time for your public VICTORY!

Luke 14:11:
"For whoever exalts himself will be humbled, and he who humbles himself will be exalted."

* * *

DOUBLE HONOR

As we come together as the body of Christ, we cover our leaders. Honoring the life of Dr. Myles Monroe! (11/10/2014)

1 Timothy 5:17:
Let the elders who rule well be counted worthy of double honor, especially those who labor in the word and doctrine.

NOTES:

TRUST GOD!

Trust God! It's already done!

Proverbs 29:25:
The fear of man brings a snare, but whoever trusts in the Lord shall be safe.

* * *

"The Lord says, 'I AM your Light and your Salvation! Be fearless! Walk by faith! My path for you is illuminated! Walk in it and receive glory!'" (Long, 2014)

* * *

UNIFY

We stand in unity and GOD brings great victory!

Ephesians 4:3:
Endeavoring to keep the unity of the Spirit in the bond of peace.

NOTES:

ARE YOU A PART OF THE NUMBER?

There is STRENGTH in numbers.
Be a part of the number.

Psalm 18:32:
*It is God who arms me with strength,
and makes my way perfect.*

* * *

"The Lord says, 'Be REVIVED today as I breathe upon you! Live by My Spirit within you! Life and life more abundantly is yours as you live in Me!'" (Long, 2014)

* * *

THE GREATEST PLAN

God's original plan is the greatest plan.

Proverbs 16:9:
A man's heart plans his way, but the LORD directs his steps.

NOTES:

"The Lord says, 'Know that I AM BREAKING the barriers that have restricted your access to My promises! Nothing will deny My manifested LOVE!'" (Long, 2014)

* * *

ARE YOU ON SOLID GROUND?

Being in Christ provides solid ground on which we stand, any other surface in this time is sinking sand.

2 Timothy 2:19 (NIV):
Nevertheless, God's solid foundation stands firm, sealed with this inscription: "The Lord knows those who are his," and, "Everyone who confesses the name of the Lord must turn away from wickedness."

NOTES:

"The Lord says, 'ARISE! I have not called you to be defeated! I have called you as more than a conqueror through My LOVE! Go forth and conquer!'" (Long, 2014)

* * *

WILLING AND OBEDIENT

When obedience goes beyond how you feel, at that point God knows He can trust you.

Isaiah 1:19-20:
If you are willing and obedient, You shall eat the good of the land.

* * *

CHANGE IT!

Focus your energy and change this world we live in. IT'S TIME FOR CHANGE!

Proverbs 16:3 (NIV):
Commit to the LORD whatever you do, and he will establish your plans.

NOTES:

HAPPY THANKSGIVING!

Great accomplishments occur when you're feeling the worst, that's why VICTORY has a really good taste.

Philippians 4:6:
Be anxious for nothing, but in everything by prayer and supplication, with thanksgiving, let your requests be made known to God;

* * *

ASK, SEEK, KNOCK

Seek your God given purpose and receive God's provision. Keep Asking, Seeking, Knocking!

Matthew 7:7:
"Ask, and it will be given to you; seek, and you will find; knock, and it will be opened to you."

"God said make room and make yourself ready!" (Stokes, 2014)

NOTES:

"We are the body of Christ! WE ARE ALL
ON THE SAME TEAM!" (Long, 2014)

THE HARVEST

The Gathering of Harvest has begun
and the Scattering has ceased.

Genesis 8:22:
"While the earth remains, seedtime and harvest, cold and heat, winter and summer, and day and night shall not cease."

Isaiah 61:7 (NIV):
Instead of your shame you will receive a double portion, and instead of disgrace you will rejoice in your inheritance. And so you will inherit a double portion in your land, and everlasting joy will be yours.

2 Corinthians 8:9 (MSG):
You are familiar with the generosity of our Master, Jesus Christ. Rich as he was, he gave it all away for us—in one stroke he became poor and we became rich.

NOTES:

Galatians 5:25 (MSG):
Since this is the kind of life we have chosen, the life of the Spirit, let us make sure that we do not just hold it as an idea in our heads or a sentiment in our hearts, but work out its implications in every detail of our lives.

Galatians 6:2-3 (MSG):
Stoop down and reach out to those who are oppressed. Share their burdens, and so complete Christ's law. If you think you are too good for that, you are badly deceived.

Psalm 75:6-7:
For exaltation comes neither from the east nor from the west nor from the south. But God is the Judge: He puts down one, and exalts another.

NOTES:

"Wherever the greatest attack is in your life is the area that God wants to bless you the most!" (Long, 2014)

* * *

INHERITANCE

The process builds character to retain the inheritance that's coming your way.

Proverbs 13:22:
A good man leaves an inheritance to his children's children, but the wealth of the sinner is stored up for the righteous.

NOTES:

WATCH THIS...

Do not be afraid. You can't lose your way; watch God's signs all throughout the day.

1 Corinthians 16:13:
Watch, stand fast in the faith, be brave, be strong.

* * *

YOU'RE INVITED

You have been INVITED into a new season. SEE YOU THERE!

Luke 5:31-32 (MSG):
Jesus heard about it and spoke up, "Who needs a doctor: the healthy or the sick? I'm here inviting outsiders, not insiders—an invitation to a changed life, changed inside and out."

NOTES:

ABUNDANT LIFE IS YOURS

Life can be amazing when you decide to live it.

John 10:10:
"The thief does not come except to steal, and to kill, and to destroy. I have come that they may have life, and that they may have it more abundantly."

* * *

YOU'RE UNSTOPPABLE!

If stopping you were easy, the devil would not be working so hard to accomplish it.

Luke 10:19:
"Behold, I give you the authority to trample on serpents and scorpions, and over all the power of the enemy, and nothing shall by any means hurt you."

NOTES:

"The Lord says, 'Your best days aren't behind, but ahead of you! Endurance has prepared you for GREATER! Receive a fresh wind for a new season.'" (Long, 2014)

* * *

"When we come together as ONE, we can accomplish anything!" (Long, 2014)

* * *

NOTES:

REJOICE!

If you're not sure about today,
remember who made this day.

Psalm 118:24:
This is the day the LORD has made.

* * *

BE GLAD

We will rejoice and be glad in it.

Psalm 9:2:
*I will be glad and rejoice in You; I will
sing praise to Your name,
O Most High.*

NOTES:

www.ingramcontent.com/pod-product-compliance
Lightning Source LLC
Chambersburg PA
CBHW070655100426
42735CB00039B/2133